Contents

Written by Isabel Thomas

Collins

Living in the clouds

Cloud forests are found on high ground.

Clouds surround the trees for much of each day!

Cloud forests are so **humid** that rain drips from each leaf all day.

They are crowded with living things.
Let's meet some!

In the treetops

Birds enjoy cloud forest feasts. This bird has found a moth to eat.

This blue hummingbird reaches deep into flowers with its long beak. Then it drinks the sweet nectar from each flower.

This **teal** lizard lurks in treetops.

It stays as still as a statue until it spies insects to eat.

Not on the menu

This little insect is bright blue!

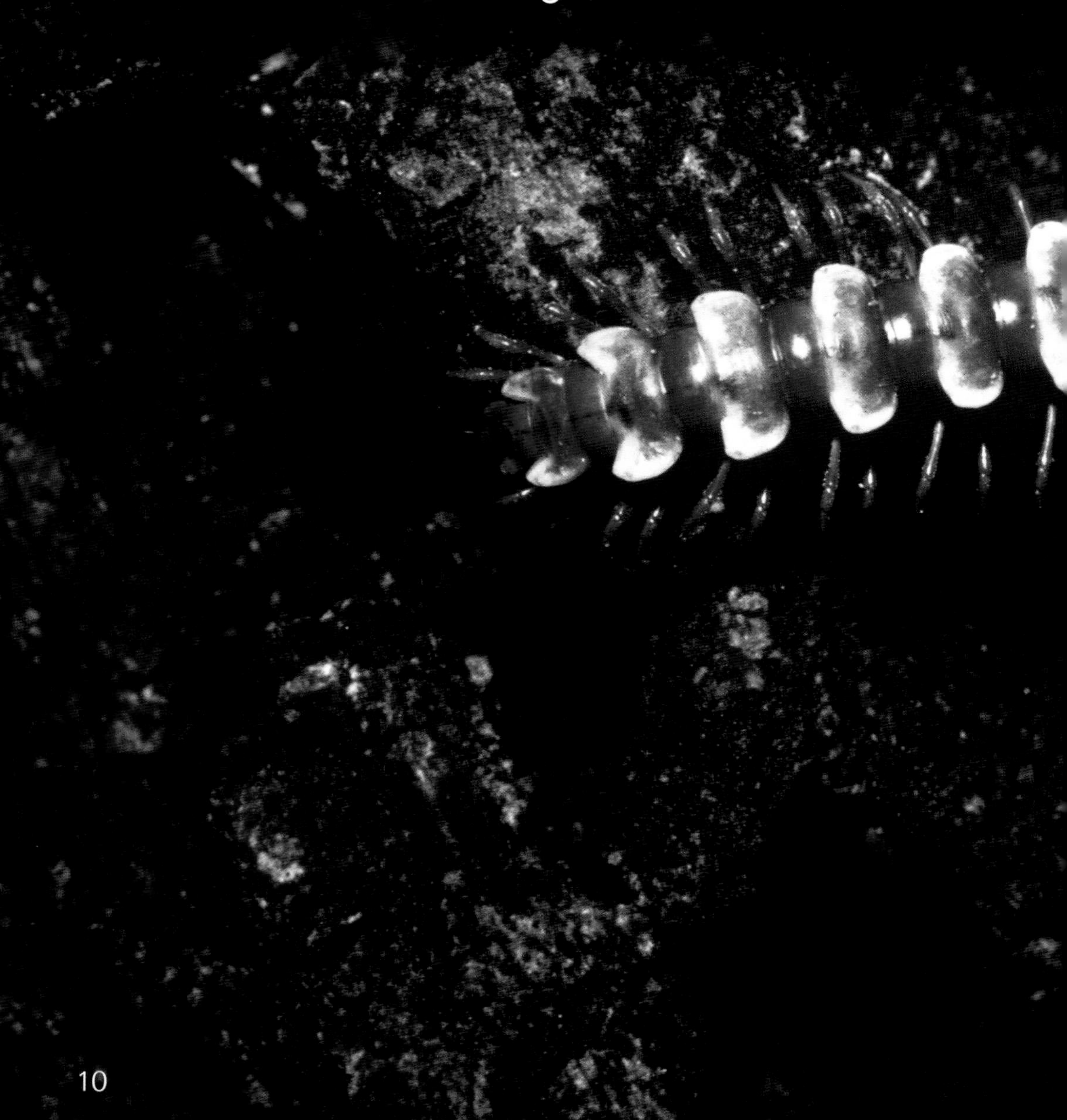

It's a **cue** for birds to stay away. It tells them that the insect is not good to eat.

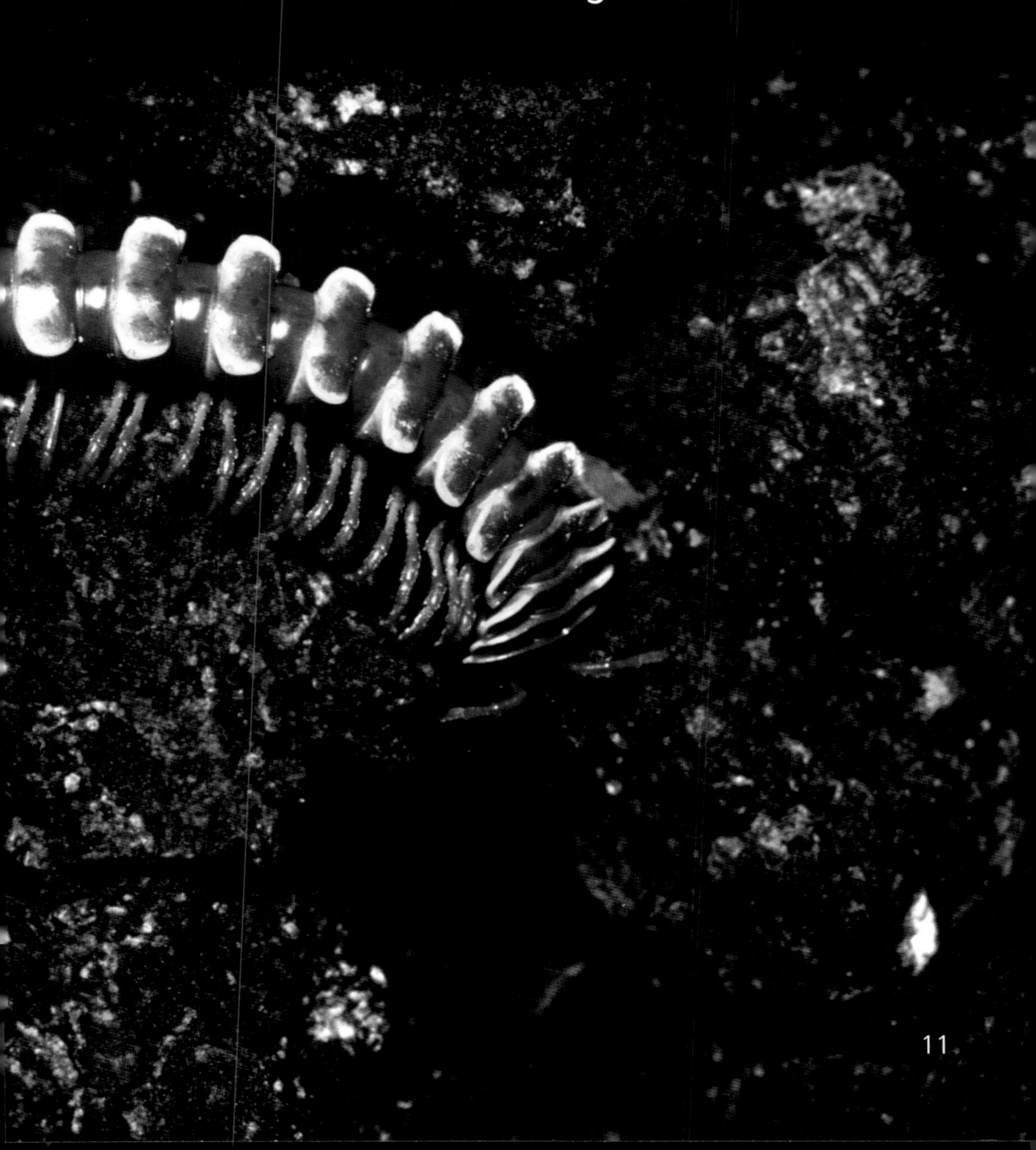

This blue jeans frog has **toxic** skin!

Just one lick can kill.

Loud and soft

Loud mandrills scream as they argue about food.

This mandrill's blue snout and bottom mean that he is the boss.

Sh! What is stirring in the dirt and leaf litter?

It’s a rainforest tarantula with electric blue legs. It patters around with a soft sound.

Valuing cloud forests

Cloud forests are full of astounding living things.

We must **value** and protect cloud forests so the living things can stay there forever.

cue prompt or hint

humid moist air

teal dark greenish blue

toxic has poison

value see that something is important

Cloud forest inhabitants

Review: After reading

Use your assessment from hearing the children read to choose any GPCs, words or tricky words that need additional practice.

Read 1: Decoding

- Help the children to read longer words with the new phonemes using the "chunking method" to sound out each syllable, blending it and then reading the whole word.
  tar/ant/u/la   val/ue   as/tound/ing   surr/ound   stirr/ing   humm/ing/bird
- Model reading with lots of expression. Ask the children to read in pairs, taking turns to read a page. Ask them to try to blend words in their heads rather than out loud.

Read 2: Prosody

- Tell the children that they are going to read pages 12 and 13 as if they were presenting a nature documentary.
- First, model reading page 12 with expression and drama. Next, let the children join in reading page 13.
- Encourage individual children to take turns to read a page to the group.

Read 3: Comprehension

- Have the children read about or seen television programmes about forests? Ask them to describe what they saw, and how they were the same or different to the cloud forest in this book.
- Turn to the back cover and read the blurb. Encourage the children to explain whether they think this is a good summary or not.
- Discuss the theme of colour in the book.
  - Look at page 10, ask: Why is the insect bright blue? (*to tell birds to stay away*)
  - Ask: What other creature might be colourful for the same reason? Why? (e.g. *the frog because it is toxic*)
- Turn to pages 22 and 23, and encourage the children to talk about the animals in the pictures. Can they remember what was special or unusual about each one?